Olympic BMX

Written by Charlotte Guillain

Collins
SCHOOLS LIBRARY SERVICE

BMX stands for bicycle motocross.

Riders race around tracks on special bikes.

Road bikes

low handlebars

eight gears

70 centimetres tall

thin tyres

BMX bikes

high handlebars

one gear

51 centimetres tall

thick tyres

Some riders do tricks.

The tricks are called BMX Freestyle.

Riders practise jumps so they can do better tricks.

Riders often fall.

Riders need to train to get fit.

running

road riding

sit-ups

Riders need:

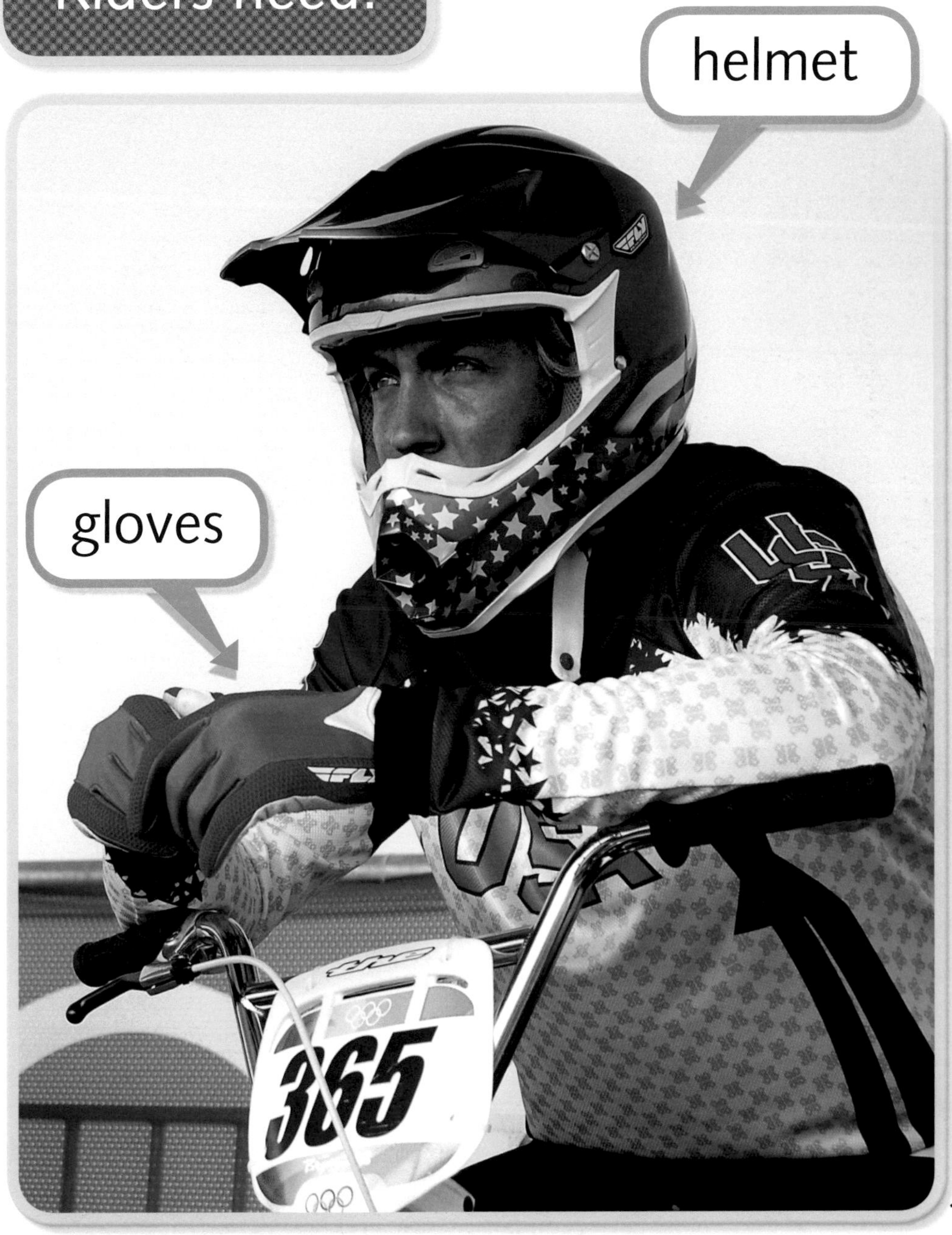

In the Olympics, riders race
on a track.

The track has jumps and bends.
The fastest rider wins a gold medal.

What riders need

helmet

gloves

bike

What riders need to do

train

jump

practise

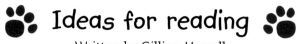

Ideas for reading

Written by Gillian Howell
Primary Literacy Consultant

Learning objectives: *(reading objectives correspond with Yellow band; all other objectives correspond with Ruby band)* read longer words including simple two and three syllable words; use phonics to read unknown or difficult words; use knowledge of different organisational features of texts to find information effectively; identify and summarise evidence from a text to support a hypothesis; interrogate texts to deepen and clarify understanding and response; choose and combine words, images and other features for particular effects

Curriculum links: P.E.: Outdoor and adventurous activities

High frequency words: some, do, one, eight, has, out, what, how, be

Interest words: Olympic, bicycle, motocross, racers, bikes, tricks, freestyle, handlebars, gears, tyres, centimetres, helmet, gloves, practise, track

Resources: paper, pens, pencils, paints, internet

Word count: 88

Getting started

- Ask the children if they have bikes and, in particular, BMX bikes. Invite some of the children to describe the sort of things they do on their bikes.

- Look together at the cover. Ask the children what they think the boy on the bike is doing. Read the title together and ask the children if they know that BMX bikes race in the Olympics and what the race would be like.

- Turn to the back cover and read the blurb together. Ask the children to say what sort of information they think will be in the book. Ask them what features non-fiction books have, e.g. photos, labels and why they are useful.

Reading and responding

- Ask the children to read the text on their own. Remind them to use their phonics knowledge to work out words they are unsure of. Prompt them to look for words within words such as *motocross* on p2 and *freestyle* on p5.

- On pp4–5, ask the children to look at the photos on both pages together and make comparisons between the two bikes. Ask them why they think the BMX bikes are different in this way.